S0-AWS-556

The

Life

Series

The
Life
Series

by Doris J. Paterson

Portage & Main Press

© 1996, Doris Paterson

All rights reserved.
No part of this publication may be
reproduced or transmitted in any form or by any means
– graphic, electronic, or mechanical –
without the prior written permission of the publisher.

Canadian Cataloguing in Publication Data

Paterson, Doris J. (Doris Joy), 1924 -
The Life series
1st ed. --
ISBN 0-9694264-3-7

1. Paterson, Doris J. (Doris Joy), 1924 -   I. Title.
ND249.P373A4 1996   759.11   C96-920154-0

Printed and bound in Canada
by Kromar Printing Limited

First Edition

Book and cover design by Nancy A. Newman

Portage & Main Press
102-318 McDermot Avenue
Winnipeg, MB, Canada R3A 0A2
toll free: 1-800-667-9673

She encourages and supports those who create
I applaud her and dedicate this book to
Mary Dixon

Introduction

Doris Paterson is a woman of great energy and formidable talent. She has had a long and interesting life to date, and is painting and writing today at a truly impressive rate and degree of excellence.

Since I first saw the paintings shown in this book, which was in January of 1995, Doris has completed some three hundred works. She is in her studio, working, virtually every day. She has done a series of ten Boulders, wonderful acrylics of big stones that manage to convey energy, spirituality, humour, and beauty. She has continued to do Goddess and Earth Mother paintings, two of which were selected, from some 800 entries, for a juried show in Taos, New Mexico. She returns from time to time to a fascination with medieval icons and has done many acrylic paintings in this particular style. She has completed many multi-media works and a series of collaged figures.

This year Doris was tempted to do something different – hardly surprising as this has driven her creativity all her life - and, with her friend and fellow artist Dorothy St. Hilaire, created at 29" X 45" fabric wall hanging based on Doris's 'Celebration,' the final painting in this book. This involved the two artists in women's traditional use of fabrics and stitchery: acquiring the fabrics, making the pattern, cutting and hand sewing. This work was shown in September of this year to great acclaim.

Most recently Doris attended a week-long workshop on Whidbey Island, off the coast of Washington with instructor Katherine Chang Lui. The previous week Doris had seen the work of the Austrian painter Hundtertwasser who, with his compatriots Klimt and Klee, uses patterns and colors in a style of sophisticated naiveté. Doris had immediately felt, as she wrote to me, a 'familiar pull in her insides' and felt inspired at the workshop to, as she put it, 'doodle around'. To her amazement and excitement, Katharine Chang Lui was very taken with these impressions. As a result, this will be Doris's direction for the next few months. I have seen photographs of some early works in this style and they are wonderful.

Untitled
egg tempera on card
7-5/8 X 10-5/16 inches / 19.37 X 26.19 cm

I met Doris nearly thirty years ago when my husband and I bought, at a juried art show in Winnipeg, a smallish, egg tempera painting, untitled, which showed the head of a girl (shown above). It has always been a favourite in our home.

While she still lived in Winnipeg, before the breakup of her marriage and her subsequent move to British Columbia, we became friends. Living on opposite sides of the city, each being involved in various undertakings, and each having the demands of a home and school-aged chidren, our meetings were not as frequent as we would have liked, but often enough to establish a bond. I admired her greatly and was able to add many of her works to our modest collection. We were particularly fond of her Japanese style woodcut prints, one of which is shown opposite (lower right), and the intaglio prints (upper right) Doris created when she had her own press.

Ballet Girls
intaglio
11 X 7-1/2 inches / 27.9 X 19.0 cm

Sunflowers
woodcut
11 X 18 inches / 27.9 X 45.7 cm

Some time after she settled in British Columbia, we corresponded about doing some children's books together, but, for various reasons, this did not happen. Undeterred, Doris wrote and illustrated a favourite story, *The Bond,* and hand-bound numerous copies for her grandchildren.

Figure 4) Lilies
tissue paper collage
14-3/4 X 40-3/4 inches / 37.46 X 103.5 cm

Around that time, along with watercolours and paintings in other media, Doris had started doing collages of hand-coloured paper that she shaped and pasted and drew upon to create florals, landscapes, and figures. Being an avid gardener and lover of flowers, many of these (shown above) have been lovingly added to our family's homes

When I visited Doris in 1995, she had done a workshop with Carole Barnes in Colorado, and was working in yet anothe medium: acrylics. She had talked about the technique and how 'natural' it felt to be working in that manner, and showed me several pieces that she had executed. These were strongly coloured, powerful works, a great departure from the gentle flowers of the last work I had seen, and of course I had to have some of these as well.

Over lunch, she let me know that she had actually done many other works in acrylic. She said she was disturbed by some of the paintings and that some of her valued regular patrons were not at all pleased with the direction of her new work and that, as a result, she had put them away. I insisted on seeing them, and from under her bed came the Life Series. I think some tears were shed that day because the works were so powerful, and told so courageous a story, that I was quite moved. My strongest emotion was that they be shared, as a discrete body of work, but more importantly, as a vivid representation of one woman's life. To discover that she had written prose poems about each of the works, and then to read them, was overwhelming. With hurried conversation (I was to drive to the airport in minutes to catch a plane) we made the first tentative plans to 'do a book'.

Since that time, we have not only undertaken this, but arranged gallery showings of the work, published three limited edition prints and, for greater sharing of the work at affordable prices, produced many posters and cards. We have also published Doris' *Willy and Me*, a new edition of her self-published *The Willy Stories*. I am delighted to be a part of this display of a prodigious talent and a truly admirable woman.

The story of Doris Paterson's life is well told in her own words in the pages that follow, and her chronological biography includes the busy-ness of her 'other' non-artist self. She is a role model for any creative woman who must juggle the demands of her art – whatever the form – and the demands of a full time wife/mother/homemaker. Doris paints almost every day, yet has time for an active and interesting life with Willy, and for keeping in touch with her legion of friends and a very large family. She enjoys the affection of a large number of art collectors, and sells her work almost as fast as she can produce it. At seventy-two, Doris is happy, creative, vivacious, in good health for her age, in love with Willy, and in love with life. It is a privilege to introduce her to you.

Mary Dixon
Publisher

CHRONOLOGY

July 9th, 1924   Born Doris Joy Pearce in Gosport, near Portsmouth, England

Father was a member of the Royal Engineers in the British Army, and the family was posted to various locations, including the following:

1928 to 1930	Ireland
1930 to 1936	London, Guilford, Tidworth, England
1936 to 1939	Kowloon and Hong Kong, China
1939 to 1946	Hempstead, Warwickshire, England
1946	married to a Canadian airman and immigrated to Canada as a war bride
1946 to 1950	Cornwall, Ontario
1948	first child born, converts to Catholicism
1949	second child born
1950 to 1954	Sudbury, Ontario
1951	third child born, studied leather and copper-tooling
1954 to 1957	North Bay, Ontario
1954	fourth child born, studied oil painting at night school
1957 to 1959	Trois Rivière, Quebec
1957	fifth child born, studied sculpture
1958	sixth child born
1959 to 1960	Rimouski, Quebec
1960 to 1962	Summerside, Prince Edward Island
1961	studied portrait oil painting, won first award in jury show
1962 to 1966	Edmonton, Alberta
1962	seventh child born
1963	took private lessons in pastel, specializing in portraits, accepted portrait commissions, studied figure drawing and painting at University of Alberta extension courses workshop with Alex Colville
1964	eighth child born
1966 to 1968	Winnipeg, Manitoba
1966	joined Winnipeg Sketch Club, ninth child born
1967	tenth child born
1968 to 1969	Ottawa, Ontario
1968	worked in oil paints, focusing on figures and portraits
1969	studied in Toronto, Three Schools courses

1970 to 1975	Mississauga, Ontario
	won awards in juried shows
1975 to 1982	Winnipeg, Manitoba
	founding member of Medea Gallery
	Art Forum, Norman Art Group, Symposium of Art
	studied printmaking (woodcuts, etchings, dry point, silkscreen)
	won awards in local shows
	workshop with Clement Greenberg
	studied woodcuts with Toshi Yoshida in Japan
	tour of New York
1976	marriage breakdown, separation
	children then 28, 27, 25, 22, 19, 18, 14, 12, 10, 9
1981	divorce
1982	solo show at Medea Gallery, Winnipeg
1982 to 1987	Nanaimo, British Columbia
	studied sculpture, lithography, drawing, clay at Malaspina College
	independent studies with Robin Field
	first prize in Images and Objects
	awards in regional shows
	worked in watercolour
	founding member of Art 10 Gallery
1985	solo show at Old Mahle House Gallery, Cedar, British Columbia
1987 to 1988	Clearbrook, British Columbia
1987	joined Fraser Valley Graphic Group,
	Federation of Artists, Vancouver
	workshop with Edward Betts
	worked in treated paper and collage
1987	solo show at Malaspina Gallery, Nanaimo, British Columbia
1988 -	Mission, British Columbia
1988	joined Mission Artist Association, Vancouver Federation of Artists
	workshop with Carla O'Conner
	workshop with Carole Barnes
	wrote, illustrated, and self-published *The Willy Stories*
	founding member of Fine Arts Five
1989	solo show at New Westminister Library Gallery
1989	solo show at Arts Council Gallery, Mission,B.C.
1994	solo show at Gateway Theatre Gallery, Richmond, B.C.
1995	two works accepted for juried group show in Taos, New Mexico
1993 - 1996	created majority of paintings in the Life Series
1996	first reproductions of work, Life Series book published.

Baby

A family story:
>Nurses put me in the solarium
>to get some sun.

When my father first saw me
>I was as red as a pomegranate
>and he said to my mother,
>"Does this ugly duckling *really* belong to us?"

Baby, 1983
oil on stretched canvas
16 X 20 inches / 40.6 X 50.8 cm

Convent

At my convent school in Hong Kong
        the nuns had come from Paris
        with cultivated tastes,
        refined demeanour,
        and musical, sensuous language.

Their dedication was both to educate
        the students and bring
        more Catholics into the fold.

At night they searched the streets
        for girl babies left in gutters.
        The adjoining orphanage
        brought them up
        trained in sewing and housework
        so they could be employed
        as Ahmahs (servants)
        for British families.

Convent, 1994
acrylic on paper
22 X 30 inches / 55.9 X 76.2 cm

Alice

The only events
>   staged on the island of Hong Kong
>   between 1936 and 1939 were the productions
>   put on by the sisters. The stage sets
>   were intricately designed and painted.
>   Brilliant costumes were created
>   by the orphanage ladies.

In *Alice* the Griffin was covered with scales
>   and greatly winged. The Queen of Hearts
>   was imposing in her taffeta white dress
>   with large red hearts.

I played Alice, a picture-book blue-eyed blonde
>   amongst the dark-haired Chinese and Filipino girls.
>   The chief seamstress had no arms
>   but sat on a low table
>   to fit my dresses, swivelling her torso
>   and picking up pins with her toes.

Exams were excused while I rehearsed.
>   I left the girls with furrowed brows in the classroom
>   while I stepped into fantasy land. I loved
>   the exhilaration of performing and gloried in being
>   a favoured person.

My father was flummoxed. His daughter
>   was supposed to shine in academics but I
>   shone in the footlights instead.

Alice, 1993
acrylic on paper
30-1/4 X 22-3/4 inches / 76.8 X 57.8 cm

Cinderella Dress

When I played Cinderella.
      My ball gown was white satin
      with frills and flounces
      over a great crinoline.

The armless seamstress had sewn pearls
      onto the bodice and tucked
      small, pink rosebuds into the neckline.
      She made me into a princess.

When I made my entrance
      onto the stage, the audience gasped
      and applauded.

After the production, the Reverend Mother
      took me into her oak-panelled office.

"Dorice," she said, "If you will become a Catholic,
      we will give you Cinderella's ball gown."

I was fourteen years old.

Cinderella Dress, 1993
acrylic on paper
30 X 22 inches / 76.2 X 55.9 cm

Warwick Castle

British Iron and Steel Corporation
        took over Warwick Castle during the war.

I worked in Queen Anne's bedroom
        as a typist who rarely typed.
        Again, I was excused
        because I was the lead in local plays.
        Noel Coward's pieces, and *Hobson's Choice,*
        and *Pride and Prejudice.*

But we all did "fire-watch" duty in the castle,
        checking for conflagrations
        after fire bombs were dropped
        by unmanned enemy aircraft.
        Swapping horror stories, we toured the dungeons
        and stone towers. One of the girls
        saw an apparition and became hysterical.

Now Warwick Castle is perfectly preserved,
        with Madame Tussaud wax figures
        in frozen portrayals of life in those times.

Warwick Castle, 1993
acrylic and collage on paper
22 X 30 inches / 55.9 X 76.2 cm

Queen for a Day

Leamington Spa is a good-sized town
in Warwickshire. At a dance
in the town hall, my friends
pushed me into the contest
for Beauty Queen.

I had visions of my father's disapproval.
Ladies did not put themselves
on display.
But I did it anyway, preening in my
short, flowered, many-coloured
dress of Egyptian cotton.

A male film-star with greasy hair anointed me
with a kiss, declared me the winner,
and presented me with a silver chalice.

Next day, prim, middle-aged spinsters
clucked disapprovingly,
accused me of being "cheap".
I resigned my position.

Queen for a Day, 1993
acrylic on paper
30 X 22 inches / 76.2 X 55.9 cm

Alice Blue Gown

I met him at a dance.
        I was wearing my Alice Blue gown,
        with the skirt that flared,
        showing my shapely legs.

He was like his country,
        clean, idealistic and open.
        The colour of his eyes
        matched my dress.

We danced and we twirled.
        And we thought that life together
        would be like that dance,
        that there would always be music
        and stars in our eyes.

Alice Blue Gown, 1994
acrylic on paper
30-1/4 X 22-3/4 inches / 76.8 X 57.8 cm

Wedding

We married in a Catholic church
      in Rochester, Kent.
      We couldn't have a mass
      because I wasn't Catholic.

No coupons for clothes,
      I wore a borrowed wedding dress.
      My family sacrificed their sugar
      and butter rations for the wedding cake.

At first my father refused
      to give me away.
      In his mind, no one
      was good enough for his daughter.
      We told him not to be an 'old poop',
      and he relented.

Wedding, 1994
acrylic on paper
20-1/4 X 24 inches / 51.4 X 61 cm

Landed Immigrant

The pull of what's safe, known
      and loved
      against the magnet
      of the new and possible.

Instead of my roles in theatre,
      our home will be my new stage.

My man waits for me.
      He is the gateway
      to new experience.

For now, doubts
      must stay quiet – I go
      through the doorway
      to new beginnings.

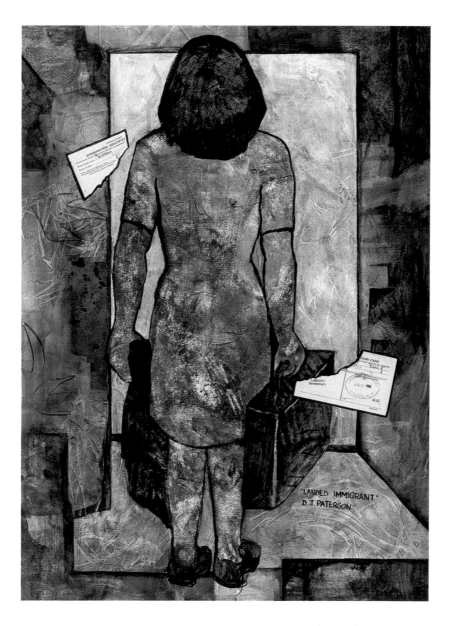

Landed Immigrant, 1994
acrylic and collage on paper
30 X 22 inches / 76.2 X 55.9 cm

To Be or Not To Be

Every day I waited
        for my husband to come home
        from his work and ease
        my loneliness.

Pacing our near-empty house
        back and forth, I felt like a moth
        batting against a light.

Winter's cold fingers touched all around me.
        Sheets froze on the line. I brought them inside
        to thaw. They stood near the walls
        like stiff ghosts, breathing
        their misty breaths until they softened
        and collapsed in heaps.

Then I was pregnant.
        My mother-in-law brought me yards
        of flannelette from the cotton mill
        so that I could sew diapers. I wanted
        this baby to bring warmth to my life
        and give me roots.

To Be or Not To Be, 1993
acrylic on paper
22 X 28-1/2 inches / 55.9 X 72.4 cm

Limbo

I didn't know the baby
        had lived for two hours.
        Stunned, I didn't ask where it was.

The sisters said they baptized her
        so she could be registered Catholic
        and buried in hallowed ground.

Unbaptized babies go to Limbo, they told me,
        neither heaven nor hell,
        merely an empty space between.
        Perpetual nothing.

As we were leaving the hospital,
        a nun presented us with a shoe-box.
        The dead baby was in it.

Limbo, 1993
acrylic on paper
22 X 28-1/2 inches / 55.9 X 72.4 cm

Confessional

It was plain things weren't working out.
     My Mother-in-law
     had never wanted a Protestant anywhere near her.
     I was still an outsider.
     So I made a vow.
     If God would give me a baby
     I would become a Catholic.

To embrace the Catholic religion
     I went to confession.
     A priest sat behind the dimly-lit grill
     in a small, confined structure
     like a shoe-box tipped on end.
     The place was suffocating,
     filled with heartaches
     and spilled-over sins.

Confessional, 1990
mixed media on card
13-3/8 X 17 inches / 33.9 X 43.2 cm

Birth

Pushed into this world with a scream
        she was born, giving meaning
        to my life.

My mother-in-law
        softened when she saw the little one
        had a small hole in the lobe of her left ear,
        the same as her father.
        And her grandmother.

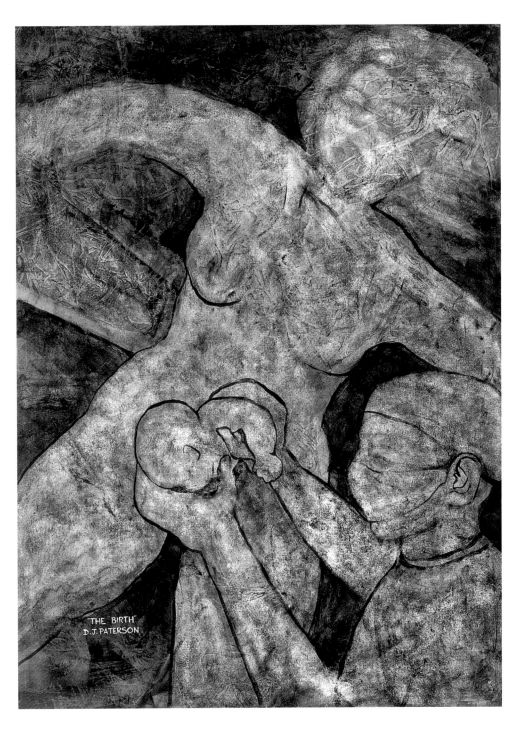

The Birth
D.J.PATERSON

Birth, 1993
acrylic on paper
30 X 22 inches / 76.2 X 55.9 cm

Mother

I am mother ten times over.
        I believed that my pregnancies
        were God's will
        and accepted them whole-heartedly.

In return, I believed
        He
        would care for us.

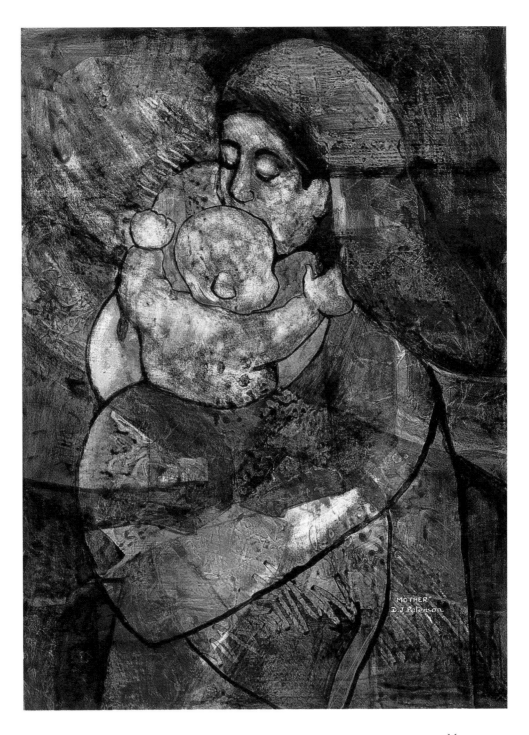

Mother, 1992
acrylic on paper
30 X 22 inches / 76.2 X 55.9 cm

The Shower

We had moved Prince Edward Island to Edmonton,
      or that's how it seemed, travelling
      with our six children, our daily necessities stowed
      in a gypsy plywood box on the roof of the car.

Six months on the prairies, five months pregnant,
      I was taken to the hospital.
      In the silent heart of the night
      baby Warren was born in my bed. A nurse's aide
      came running, whispering the rules of the hospital,
      said she couldn't leave my side to get the doctor
      before the placenta came.

"Baptize him," I cried. "Get water from the sink."
      "I can't do it", she said at first,
      thinking of rules again, church rules.
      But she did. I heard in the still, dark hospital
      "I baptize thee in the name of the Father
      and of the Son and of the Holy Ghost."
      "Amen," I said, feeling better.
      "Amen," she echoed.

Warren didn't live.

For our seventh child,
      my friend took a photo of the shower.

The Shower, 1991
mixed media on board
16 X 20 inches / 40.6 X 50.8 cm

Art Teacher

I've always drawn, always painted
      as a youngster, as a teen, as a young woman.

Married, wherever we moved, I reached for my paints.
      I was always eager for new teachers, art lessons.

Once I thought I'd be a portrait artist,
      made some money with pastels.
      But mothers insisted their daughters look
      younger, prettier, and thirty pounds lighter.
      And official portraits of politicians had to replicate
      the other dark faces in the legislative hallways.

It cramped my style, my excitement with paint.
      So I resisted these commissions, and art became
      simply
      my life-raft.

Art Teacher, 1991
mixed media on board
20 X 16 inches / 50.8 X 40.6 cm

Art Critic

Twenty artists invited
     Clement Greenberg to Winnipeg.
     He told us we were just as valid as
     New York artists.

We went to see for ourselves,
     visiting his apartment
     in New York City the following year.
     It was filled with the work of the Modern Masters.

His words to me: "You're looking for the key,
     but there isn't one."

Art Critic, 1991
mixed media on board
16 X 20 inches / 40.6 X 50.8 cm

Learning Woodcuts in Japan

I was doing western-type woodcuts, but yearned
    to practice the Japanese style,
    using rice paste and powdered pigments,
    rubbing with an intricately woven baren.

Noburu Sawaii arrived in Winnipeg, burdened as a mule
    with tools, paper and films for our workshop.
    Two years later his master opened a school in Japan.
    We had to find fifteen people with
    three thousand dollars and six weeks to spare
    to study under Toshi Yoshida.
    We did it.

The gifted musician Kitaro was at the centre. I admired
    his discipline and his music:
    a strange beauty of classical instruments
    woven together by an electronic net.

Too involved with my work, I didn't attend the closing party.
    It was more important to cut my blocks.
    I sat alone, chipping away. Kitaro
    led the party-goers down the corridors, playing his guitar.
    He hopped onto the table
    next to mine, serenading and saluting
    another disciplined soul.

My prints had the same spirit as his music, he said.

Learning Woodcuts in Japan, 1995
mixed media on card
20 X 24 inches / 50.8 X 61 cm

Send in the Clowns

Fearing he couldn't cope with business stress
      I made the home front run smoothly.

The children couldn't wait
      for late dinner hours
      and he couldn't stand the noise
      and spilt milk.

Resentment smouldered and
      I started to smoke secretly, snuffing out butts
      in squares of aluminum foil
      when I heard him in the driveway.

Art life quickened for me,
      filling the void
      of his absence, his working late nights
      and of course, the volleyball games.

And he joined the busy, busy
      businessmen, running to meetings
      and conferences with their briefcases
      and importance. Forgetting family life.

Send in the Clowns, 1993
acrylic on paper
30 X 22 inches / 76.2 X 55.9 cm

Things Will Be Different Now

Is there any use to say the why of it?
      We knew the end was coming.

Like Pandora, I couldn't close the box.
      My eyes were open to see too wide a chasm
      to ever cross again; we separated.

When the day came for him to take his clothes
      from our closet, and close
      the front door for the last time,
      it was shocking.

He was torn with regret
      but feeling free.
      I was determined to keep my head high
      but anguish lay beneath the surface.

Alimony came with regularity.
      There was no going back.

Things Will Be Different Now, c.1990
mixed media on board
20 X 16 inches / 50.8 X 40.6 cm

Labyrinth

The night I reached the far end
       of my agony, I went down on my knees.
       Everything had collapsed – there seemed to be
       no answer, no hope.
       I heard an awful moaning
       and realized that the sound was
       coming from me.

Down, down into the labyrinth.
       I had to search through the pain
       so that I could heal and resurface
       a stronger woman.

I didn't know that then.

Labyrinth, 1994
mixed media on card
17-1/2 X 22-3/4 inches / 44.5 X 57.8 cm

Empty Nest

The days give me the freedom
    to fly to my work. Possibility
    becomes real; I take courses
    in clay work and lithography.

And yet.
    I used to be the centre
    of life in the home – children's voices,
    the clatter of mealtimes, the comings and goings
    to schools, dates, sports. Arguments,
    teasing, television, and music practice:
    French horn, clarinet, flute
    and yes, even drums.

Now there are only echoes.
    The children are grown, leaving
    an empty shell of a mother
    bereft
    of a time that will not come again.

Within the artwork:
"The Empty Nest"
D.J.Paterson

Empty Nest, 1994
acrylic on paper
30 X 22 inches / 76.2 X 55.9 cm

Sir Willy to the Rescue

Stuck in an apartment
     without a car to transport paintings,
     I felt like giving up my work.

Willy found me.
     Used his truck to load my watercolours
     and oils, my canvasses,
     my work all framed for shows,
     with glass and without.
     He rescued me and my art-life.

He is known to be inseparable from his bike.

Sir Willy to the Rescue, 1994
acrylic on paper
22 X 30 inches / 55.9 X 76.2 cm

Willy and Me

As I lived the experience
> of connecting to someone so opposite
> to myself, I wrote it all down.

I laughed at his wit.
> Melted with his sweetness
> Fumed at his stubbornness
> and frugality. Suspecting him
> of solitary drinking, I slurped a taste
> from a suspicious bottle. It looked like vodka;
> it was liquid floor polish!

I accused him of being stingy;
> he took me to Birk's and bought me an opal ring
> surrounded by diamonds.

Finally, we accepted each other's flaws.
> And we celebrate
> our appreciation of being together.

I printed the book myself, named it
> *The Willy Stories,*
> and sold three hundred copies.

Willy and Me, 1994
acrylic on paper
30 X 22 inches / 76.2 X 55.9 cm

Writing

For years streams of words
       and poured-out feelings
       flooded my letters to friends and family back home.
       Looking back, they must have dreaded
       wading through.

Later, when I was alone,
       one daughter suggested I make copies
       of the hundreds of letters. Would it lead
       to writing personal essays, journal stories?
       Another daughter paid to rent
       the heavy, black Olivetti.
       I joined writers' groups and finally succumbed to
       Revision!

I still write pieces about my life, some short fiction.
       This occupation (preoccupation?)
       ferries me to and from my painting.

Writing, 1994
acrylic on paper
22 X 30 inches / 55.9 X 76.2 cm

Hawaii

For our first vacation out of the country,
        Willy had found a Valentine-red
        bathing suit. He put hundred dollar bills
        in a condom and pinned it to the inside pocket -
        a waterproof safe!

Willy let me do my "t'ing." I visited
        the Art Gallery and library alone,
        absorbing Hawaiian history, without haste.

I loved the lushness of that island, the gentle
        warm ways of its people – the sensation
        was one of relaxing.

When we got home, I realized
        it had been a honeymoon!

Hawaii, 1994
acrylic on paper
22 X 30 inches / 55.9 X 76.2 cm

Camellia

Took her first steps when she visited Gram.
    We share a bond,
    Camellia and I.

I wrote and illustrated a picture book
    about the bond, putting it together by hand.

I made fourteen copies,
    one for each grandchild.

Camellia, c 1990
mixed media on card
13-1/4 X 17-1/2 inches / 33.6 X 44.5 cm

Family Negative

Oh! that I could say families
      pull together and love one another
      as shown through the camera's lens.

But there are hurts, divisions, accusations,
      and no forgiving. An image so torn
      a mother cannot piece it together.

And the negative
      stays negative.

Family Negative, 1994
mixed media on card
17-1/2 X 22-3/4 inches / 44.5 X 57.8 cm

Puck

The nick-name
        for someone who encouraged
        and believed in me.

And bought my paintings
        with cold hard cash.

Puck, 1994
acrylic on paper
15-1/4 X 16-3/4 inches / 38.7 X 42.5 cm

Peggy's Garden

Willy paid for me to visit my sister
      in England
      the summer before she was ill.

As I worked on this piece,
      it looked like a garden but
      I was filled with grief.

I cut out the sketch I had made of Peggy's patio
      and collaged the plants and table and chair,
      all the scraps that remained to memory.

The image seemed to bring her close.
      Still, she had died.

Peggy's Garden, 1994
mixed media on card
22-3/4 X 30-1/4 inches / 57.8 X 76.8 cm

New Beginnings

Layer on layer
      of acrylic colour. Shapes
      on shapes.

Meditation.
      And concentration
      dismisses the conscious will.

Images emerge, sometimes frightening,
      telling me of times I don't want to confront again.
      A face appears, compelling,
      unnerving, insisting it stay on the paper,
      surfacing through my attempts to obliterate it.

Someone comes to buy the one with the riveting face,
      as though drawn by a magnetic field. He senses
      the image cannot rest until its story is told.

This way of working brings me to a new plateau.
      There are always new beginnings.

Dawn / New Beginnings, 1994
acrylic on paper
22 X 30 inches / 55.9 X 76.2 cm

Search for Self

I'm beginning to understand
      more about myself.

No longer confined to former roles
      I can agree when someone suggests I am
      a role-model
      for other women. None of it is deliberate,
      no attempt of mine to make an impression.
      My art makes itself – with my help.

Showing my work is a search for validation.
      It is necessary as breathing
      to not have people turn their backs to me,
      waving my paintings away.

Search for Self, 1994
acrylic on paper
22 X 30 inches / 55.9 X 76.2 cm

70th Birthday

My children gave me a 70th birthday party.
      Afterward, my painting showed a face
      and a crown.

Close to me, weighted to the floor
      was the balloon saying,
         "Still perfect after seventy years!"

70th Birthday, 1994
acrylic, mixed media collage on paper
30 X 22 inches / 76.2 X 55.9 cm

Celebration

I thought *Birthday* was the last work
      of the "Life Series." More paintings
      surface, prove me wrong.
      Like life itself, the canvasses pile up –
      so different –
      I stack these emotional turning points
      beneath the bed, pulling them out,
      occasionally,
      to show some visitors.

My new work grows
      and it grows more personal.
      When it moves me, will it touch others?

Celebration, 1994
acrylic on paper
30 X 22 inches / 76.2 X 55.9 cm